D1710072

THE WORLD OF MYTHOLOGY:
EUROPEAN MYTHOLOGY

BY JIM OLLHOFF

VISIT US AT
WWW.ABDOPUBLISHING.COM

Published by ABDO Publishing Company, 8000 West 78th Street, Suite 310, Edina, MN 55439. Copyright ©2011 by Abdo Consulting Group, Inc. International copyrights reserved in all countries. No part of this book may be reproduced in any form without written permission from the publisher. ABDO & Daughters™ is a trademark and logo of ABDO Publishing Company.

Printed in the United States of America, North Mankato, Minnesota.
112010
052013

 PRINTED ON RECYCLED PAPER

Editor: John Hamilton
Graphic Design: Sue Hamilton
Cover Design: Neil Klinepier
Cover Photo: Gonzalo Ordóñez
Interior Photos and Illustrations: Alamy-pgs 26 & 27; AP-pgs 6, 7 & 19; The British Museum & Richard Neave-pg 18; Corbis-pgs 4, 5 & 16; Getty Images-pgs 11, 17, 21, 22 & 23; Granger Collection-pgs 10; iStockphoto-pgs 9, 12, 29 & border image; Library of Congress-pgs 28 & 30; Lisa Hunt-pg 25; and Thinkstock-pgs 13, 14, 15 & 20.

Library of Congress Cataloging-in-Publication Data

Ollhoff, Jim, 1959-
  European mythology / Jim Ollhoff.
     p. cm. -- (The world of mythology)
  ISBN 978-1-61714-720-3
  1. Mythology, European--Juvenile literature. I. Title.
  BL689.O45 2011
  398.2094--dc22

                    2010032586

CONTENTS

The Mighty Myth...4

Land of Many Cultures...6

The Soul of European Myths...8

Celtic Myths of the British Isles...12

The Druids...16

The Celts and Human Sacrifice...18

Celtic Afterlife...20

Celtic Goddesses...22

Finnish Myths...24

Slavic Myths...26

Influence of European Myths...28

Glossary...30

Index...32

THE MIGHTY MYTH

Tens of thousands of years ago, before there were houses, towns, or governments, many people living in the European continent used caves for shelters. There are no written records of this time, but we know a little about how these people lived because they painted on the walls of their caves. Many of the paintings show hunting scenes.

Early hunters went looking for food, hoping to kill large animals and take the meat back to the rest of the tribe. It was a dangerous journey. The hunters could sometimes be killed by their prey. Hunters were successful when the tribe worked together, and when they knew where to seek their prey.

In many European cave paintings that show hunting scenes, there is a person standing off to the side who wears a bird mask. Most likely, this is the shaman, or priest, of the tribe. People believed that by wearing the bird mask, the shaman would take on the spirit of the bird, and be able to see the places where hunting was good.

Tales of bird-man shamans are a type of myth. Myths were important to people even before recorded history. Myths tell us stories that we need to hear in order to make sense of the world. And myths are still important to people today.

A bird-man shaman.

Above: Early people painted hunting scenes on cave walls.

Land of Many Cultures

Europe is a land of many different cultures, and many different countries. This has always been true. People moved into Europe at least 25,000 years ago. They survived by living in caves and hunting animals. People began farming about 10,000 BC to 8,000 BC.

The Celtic people emerged in Europe about 1000 BC. They included many different tribes, and spoke a variety of related languages. As fierce warriors, they frequently battled other Celtic tribes. Between

Roman soldiers battled the Celtic tribes for their lands.

300 BC and 100 BC, the Romans began to push the Celts north. When the Roman Empire began to crumble in the 200s and 300s AD, the Germanic tribes moved into Europe, further pushing out the Celts. Eventually, the majority of the Celts lived in the British Isles, and the Germanic tribes held most of mainland Europe.

Celtic cultures were very rich in mythologies and stories. When they moved, they brought their myths with them. When the Germanic tribes moved in, they adopted a lot of Celtic mythology.

Above: The Celtic people were a collection of many different tribes.

THE SOUL OF EUROPEAN MYTHS

Many of the myths of ancient European peoples have been lost. People who told the myths didn't write down most of the stories. Some Roman historians wrote about some of the myths, but they rewrote the mythology to fit their own gods. For example, the ancient Celts believed in a god called Belenus, the god of the sun.

Above: Belenus, the Celtic god of the sun.

Roman writers said that the Celts worshipped Apollo—the Roman god of the sun. Then, as Christianity took hold in Northern Europe after 400 AD, many of the original mythologies were lost. However, historians and mythologists managed to piece together some of the myths from many different sources.

Many European myths told of local and household gods. These were gods that were not worshipped across the land, but instead by small groups in small locations. There might be a god of this field, or a god of that mountain, or a goddess of the river by the field. These gods were known only by people in the immediate area.

Above: A statue of Apollo, the Roman god of the sun.

Most of the local gods had no temples. If people wanted to call on the god of the river, they would go to the river. The idea of gods living in temples didn't become popular until after Roman influence.

In the British Isles, many of the gods and goddesses were very similar. Most came from the same Celtic stories. While the names changed from area to area, the basic myths all came from the early stories told by the Celts.

Like the Celts, Germanic tribes had many local and household gods. Many of the Germanic tribes had mythologies that later evolved into Norse myths. The Norse mythologies built up and expanded upon early Germanic myths.

Right: A Celtic forest deity carrying a bow and a sickle.

Above: A harpist's song magically gathers local spirits from the banks of the Lora River, Scotland.

CELTIC MYTHS OF THE BRITISH ISLES

Much of what we know about Celtic myths comes from people who wrote down the stories after 1200 AD. This was long after Christian influences caused people to abandon Celtic mythology. In fact, Christian monks wrote down and preserved many of the myths, although they sometimes added their own details.

The first group of stories is called the Mythological Cycle. It is about the gods and the beginnings of the Irish people. It includes the Book of Invasions, which attempts to write out stories of gods and other supernatural creatures that invaded Ireland long before the Celts moved in. One of the invading groups was made up of descendants of the biblical figure Noah. It was probably an addition by a Christian monk who wrote down and preserved the ancient myths, but promoted Christianity as well.

Right: The creature on the flag of Wales is said by some to represent a Celtic dragon.

Above: A Celtic cross. Christian monks wrote down many of the ancient Celtic myths, although they sometimes added their own details.

The Tuatha people are featured in the Mythological Cycle. They fought many battles, first invading and then defending their land. They were children of the goddess Danu. The Tuatha defeated armies of evil creatures. When the Celtic tribes came to the land, the Tuatha retreated deep into the forests and underground mounds. There, they became known as "leprechauns."

The second collection of mythological stories is called the Ulster Cycle. The stories tell of a war between the people of Ireland and the people of Ulster. The hero of Ulster was Cuchulain, who was the son of the god of light.

A third group of myths is called the Fionn Cycle. These stories tell about Fionn and his followers. A great hero, Fionn is portrayed as fighting gods and foretelling the future.

A fourth group of stories is called the Mabinogion. It tells about the histories and genealogies of the kings. Some are accurate, but some are not. These stories are especially interesting because they include some of the first references to King Arthur.

Above: The tales of King Arthur first appeared in ancient Celtic mythology.

Above: The Tuatha people, children of the goddess Danu, became known as leprechauns.

THE DRUIDS

The druids were believed to be the priests of the Celtic people. They studied for years to understand the spirits of the forest, and how to recite magic spells. Little is known about them because they did not keep written records. It appears that they advised kings and tribal leaders. They also led worship rituals. Since they believed that gods inhabited plants and trees, their worship rituals were usually in the forest. The Romans outlawed the druids in 54 AD.

Stonehenge is an ancient circle of rocks in England. Nobody really knows why it was built. It may have been used for religious ceremonies, or as a kind of early planetarium. Some people used to think the druids built Stonehenge. However, archeologists say that Stonehenge was built in three phases. The final phase of building was about 1600 BC. The first construction may have happened around 3000 BC. This was long before the Celts arrived. Clearly, a different group of people built Stonehenge. Exactly who built the mysterious rock circle, and why, may never be known.

Some thought druids built Stonehenge for religious purposes.

Above: Stonehenge is an ancient circle of rocks in England. Scientists are still trying to figure out why it was built.

THE CELTS AND HUMAN SACRIFICE

Roman writers of the time said that the druids conducted human sacrifices. True evidence of this is difficult to come by, since there are no written records. However, a number of bodies have been found in bogs, preserved for thousands of years. One such body was called Lindow Man, found in a peat bog called Lindow Moss, in northwest England. Perfectly preserved, right down to the contents of his stomach and his last meal, the discovery provided a window into life between the years 20 AD and 90 AD.

Lindow Man seemed to be of high status, since his fingers had no calluses associated with manual labor. He met a violent death. Some historians say he was sacrificed to the gods because of the approaching Roman army. It was believed that a human sacrifice would motivate the gods to help. Some historians speculate that Lindow Man was himself a druid, offering himself as a sacrifice.

Right: Lindow Man is displayed at The British Museum in London. Medical illustrator Richard Neave recreated Lindow Man's face.

Above: Roman soldiers stop a druid sacrifice at Stonehenge. It is unknown if druids conducted human sacrifices, since there are no written records. However, several preserved bodies, possible human sacrifices, have been found in European bogs.

CELTIC AFTERLIFE

Unfortunately, very little is known about Celtic thoughts about the afterlife. Archeologists have discovered Celtic burials, where bodies were buried with food, weapons, and even chariots. It seems likely they believed in a place where the soul of the deceased would rise and carry on a life similar to the one on earth.

Roman historians wrote that the Celts believed in reincarnation. The spirit of a person who died would wander in the underworld and then come back as the spirit of something else, either a person, plant, or animal. However, there is little evidence, outside the Roman authors, that the Celts actually believed this.

Celtic mythology sometimes discusses the "otherworld." Scholars aren't sure if this land was where the gods lived, or where the spirits of dead people went, or both. The location of the otherworld was sometimes spoken of as underground. More often it was believed to be on islands located to the west of the British Isles.

Right: Celts may have believed that the spirits of dead people could come to life in another form.

Above: Some Celtic bodies were buried with food, weapons, and even chariots.

CELTIC GODDESSES

Goddesses played a huge part in Celtic mythology. Danu was a mother goddess who helped women give birth and kept children safe.

The goddess Epona was a mother goddess as well as a protector of horses. She may have been called Macha in Irish areas, and Rhiannon in the area of Wales. The Romans combined her into their own mythology.

Above: The goddess Epona was a mother goddess as well as a protector of horses.

Female goddesses were not only deities of motherhood, but also of war, of hunting, and of the earth. In fact, some of the fiercest deities were female. The goddess Morrigan decided which warriors would die in battle. She was able to turn herself into a crow, and then fly over the battlefields of losing armies.

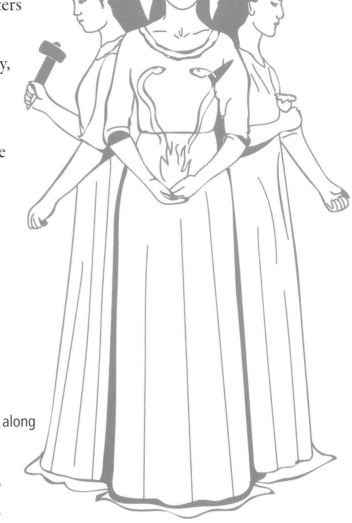

The goddess Brighid, along with her two sisters (also named Brighid), was a goddess of poetry, learning, healing, and craftsmanship. She was so popular that the Romans adopted her into their own myths.

Right: The goddess Brighid, along with her two sisters, was a goddess of poetry, learning, healing, and craftsmanship.

FINNISH MYTHS

Finland is a country to the east of Sweden. The land is heavily wooded and cold. Finnish mythology is full of forest spirits and hero stories. Like all cultures, people in Finland developed a rich set of myths.

Creation was accomplished by an air goddess named Luonnotar. As she sat one day, a duck came and landed on her knee. It laid several eggs, and then sat on them. As the eggs began to hatch, Luonnotar's knee got too hot, and she shook the eggs off. The eggs landed in the sea and became different parts of the earth and sky.

One of the god heroes of Finland is Vainamoinen, the son of Luonnotar. The air goddess was pregnant with him for 700 years. He is the god of song and poetry. Several myths tell the stories of Vainamoinen fighting evil spirits, cruel witches, and frost giantesses.

Above: Vainamoinen was the Finnish god of song and poetry.

Above: The Finnish goddess Luonnotar created different parts of the earth and sky.

SLAVIC MYTHS

The Slavic people lived in central and eastern Europe, from Poland to Siberia, stretching almost to Greece in the south. Many of the gods in Slavic mythology were local gods who ruled over a river, or a pond, or a field. Many of these local gods were mischievous. If people were lazy, the gods played tricks on them, sometimes causing accidents. If a mother were lazy, the gods would tickle her children at night so they couldn't sleep, and so the mother would have to stay up all night, too.

One of the mischievous gods was named Leshy. He was a forest spirit with a long green beard. He liked to get people lost in the forest. However, people could protect themselves from him by wearing their clothes backwards.

In some myths, the goddess of death was named Baba Yaga. She was so skinny that she looked like a skeleton with sharp teeth. Her terrifying gaze could turn people into stone. Baba Yaga also appears in Slavic folklore.

Left: A man dressed as the forest god Leshy.

Above: Baba Yaga was the goddess of death.

INFLUENCE OF EUROPEAN MYTHS

The Celtic festival of Samhain marked the end of the harvest and the beginning of winter. During this time, as plants began to die, people believed that the doorway to the underworld would open, and that the spirits of the dead would become visible. People would wear masks to make the spirits more comfortable. Later on, the Christian church celebrated their saints with All Saints' Day, also called All Hallows' Day. The night before was called All Hallows' Eve. The church wanted to Christianize pagan holidays, so they celebrated All Hallows' Eve during the Celtic festival of Samhain. Today, we know the holiday as Halloween.

The mythologies of Europe remain with us in the modern world. Stories such as King Arthur and Robin Hood have always been popular, and are still told today. Many historians believe that the mythology of King Arthur and Robin Hood began with real people, but each generation expanded the stories and added their own details. In a time when life can be chaotic and cruel, people always love these stories of courage and honor.

Right: Stories from Europe, such as Robin Hood, are still told today.

Above: During the Celtic festival of Samhain, Scottish men would darken their faces or wear masks, then dress in white to make the spirits more comfortable.

GLOSSARY

CELTIC PEOPLE

A loose-knit group of tribes that inhabited much of Europe. They were pushed to the British Isles by the Romans and later by Germanic tribes.

DRUIDS

The priests of Celtic religion.

KING ARTHUR

The legendary warrior-king of the Britons who lived in the city of Camelot and ruled with his Knights of the Round Table.

LINDOW MAN

The perfectly preserved body of a man, thrown into a bog in northwest England between the years 20 AD and 90 AD.

OTHERWORLD

The Celtic place where the gods live, and probably where the souls of the deceased reside.

PAGAN

A person who doesn't practice a widely recognized religion, such as Christianity, Judaism, or Islam. There are several definitions of the word pagan. In this book, pagans are people who worship nature or the earth, such as druids or witches.

PEAT BOG

A kind of wetland. Lots of dead plant material, called peat, builds up in the water. This makes the water mildly acidic, which kills bacteria. Also, oxygen is used up in bogs, which slows decay. Bodies buried in bogs stay very well preserved.

REINCARNATION

The belief that when people die, only their physical bodies die. The spirits of people never die, but are simply born into new bodies.

ROBIN HOOD

A legendary English hero and outlaw, who was known for taking from the rich to give to the poor.

SAMHAIN

A Celtic festival marking the beginning of winter. In modern times, the festival is known as "Halloween."

SHAMANS

People who perform an ancient form of magic called shamanism. They used a special knowledge of nature to help their tribes. Shamans believed they could heal, communicate with plants and animals, and walk between this world and the mystical world. Shamans often went into deep trances to perform their magic.

INDEX

A

All Hallows' Day 28
All Hallows' Eve 28
All Saints' Day 28
Apollo 8

B

Baba Yaga 26
Belenus 8
Book of Invasions 12
Brighid 23
Brighid (two sisters of the goddess Brighid with the same name) 23
British Isles 6, 10, 20

C

Celts 6, 8, 10, 12, 16, 20
Christianity 8, 12
Cuchulain 14

D

Danu 14, 22
druids 16, 18

E

England 16, 18
Epona 22
Europe 6, 8, 26, 28

F

Finland 24
Fionn 14
Fionn Cycle 14

G

Germanic tribes 6, 10
Greece 26

H

Halloween 28

I

Ireland 12, 14
Irish 12, 22

K

King Arthur 14, 28

L

leprechauns 14
Leshy 26
Lindow Man 18
Lindow Moss 18
Luonnotar 24

M

Mabinogion 14
Macha 22
Morrigan 23
Mythological Cycle 12, 14

N

Noah 12
Norse 10

O

otherworld 20

P

peat bog 18
Poland 26

R

reincarnation 20
Rhiannon 22
Robin Hood 28
Roman Empire 6
Romans 6, 8, 10, 16, 18, 20, 22, 23

S

Samhain 28
shaman 4
Siberia 26
Slavic people 26
Stonehenge 16
Sweden 24

T

Tuatha 14

U

Ulster 14
Ulster Cycle 14
underworld 20, 28

V

Vainamoinen 24

W

Wales 22